Pulleys

by Anne Welsbacher

Consultant:
Philip W. Hammer, Ph.D.
Assistant Manager of Education
American Institute of Physics

Bridgestone Books
an imprint of Capstone Press
Mankato, Minnesota

Bridgestone Books are published by Capstone Press
151 Good Counsel Drive, P.O. Box 669, Mankato, Minnesota 56002
http://www.capstone-press.com

Library of Congress Cataloging-in-Publication Data
Welsbacher, Anne, 1955–
    Pulleys/by Anne Welsbacher.
    p. cm.—(The Bridgestone Science Library)
    Includes bibliographical references and index.
    Summary: Uses everyday examples to describe pulleys as simple machines that make
lifting, pulling, and moving easier.
    ISBN 0-7368-0612-1
    1. Pulleys—Juvenile literature. [1. Pulleys.] I. Title. II. Series.
TJ1103.W45 2001
621.8'11—dc21
                                                                                    00-025749

Editorial Credits
Rebecca Glaser, editor; Linda Clavel, cover designer; Kia Bielke, illustrator; Katy Kudela,
    photo researcher

Photo Credits
Colephoto/Michael Caristo, 16
Dario Perla, 14
David F. Clobes, 8, 20
Shaffer Photography/James L. Shaffer, cover
Unicorn Stock Photos/Eric R. Berndt, 10
Visuals Unlimited/Mark E. Gibson, 4

1 2 3 4 5 6 06 05 04 03 02 01

Table of Contents

Simple Machines

Simple machines make work easier or faster. Work is using force to move an object across a distance. Moving, lifting, and pulling are kinds of work. Pulleys are simple machines that help make these types of work easier.

force
anything that changes the speed, direction, or motion of an object

5

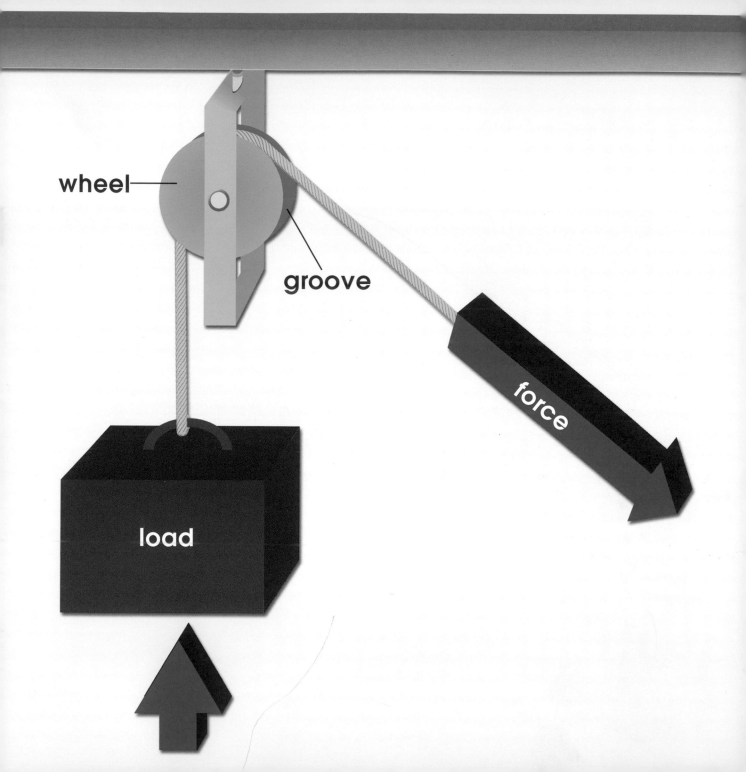

Parts of a Pulley

A pulley is a wheel with a groove that holds a rope or a chain. The groove in the wheel keeps the rope or chain in place. Pulleys help lift loads. A person pulls one end of the rope. This force lifts the load on the other end.

pulley

Single Fixed Pulleys

A single fixed pulley is attached to an object. This type of pulley changes the direction a load moves. A flagpole has a single fixed pulley. Pulling down on the rope raises the flag. Moving the rope in the opposite direction lowers the flag.

moveable pulley

Moveable Pulleys

Moveable pulleys are attached to the load instead of another object. Moveable pulleys make lifting things easier. Moveable pulleys often are used with fixed pulleys. Cranes use fixed and moveable pulleys to lift loads.

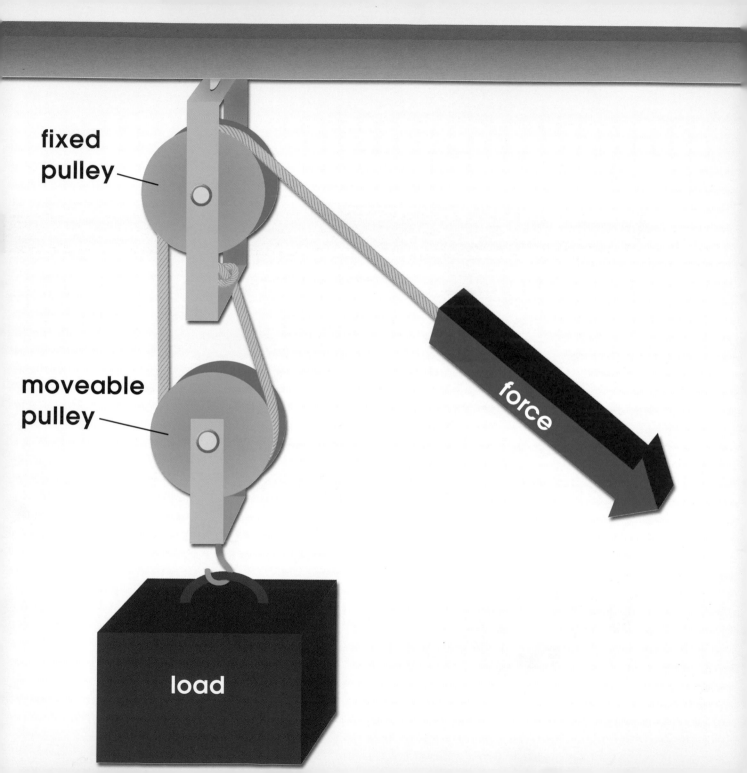

Double Pulleys

A double pulley has two pulleys. The rope is attached to a fixed pulley. The rope winds around a moveable pulley and back over the fixed pulley. Lifting a load with a double pulley is twice as easy. But the load travels only half as far.

counterweight

pulley

Counterweights

Big machines use pulleys to lift heavy loads. They also use counterweights to balance the load. Counterweights keep the machines from falling over. Large cranes that lift building parts use pulleys and counterweights.

counterweight
a weight that balances a load

Block and Tackle

A block and tackle has several fixed and moveable pulleys. The fixed pulleys are attached to a boom. The moveable pulleys are attached to the load. A rope winds around all the wheels. Loads are easier to lift because several sections of rope support the load.

boom
a fixed pole or beam

17

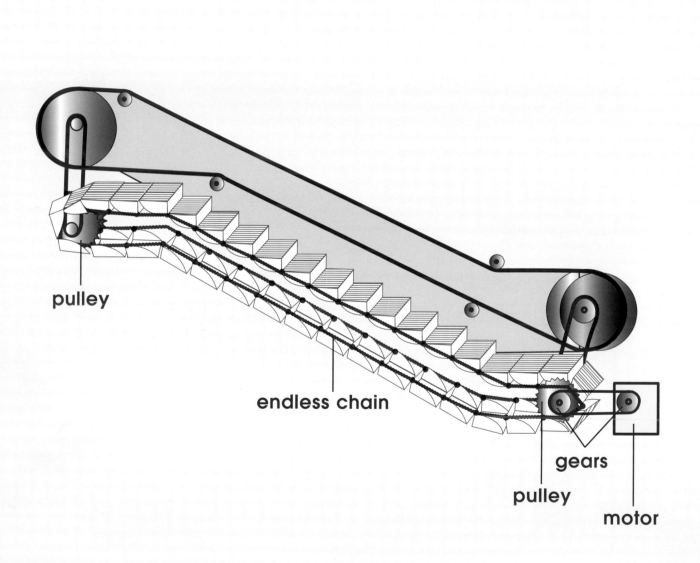

pulley

endless chain

gears

pulley

motor

Complex Machines

Simple machines can be part of complex machines. An escalator has pulleys at the top and the bottom. A loop called an endless chain connects the pulleys. A motor turns gears that move the endless chain. The stairs then move. The stairs are an inclined plane.

inclined plane
a simple machine used to move an object up or down

electric motor

pulley

counterweight

ELEVATOR

Pulleys in Elevators

People ride elevators to get to other floors of buildings. An elevator is a complex machine with many parts. Pulleys help raise and lower an elevator car. A counterweight balances the weight of the car. Electric motors produce force that turns the pulleys.

Hands On: Make an Elevator

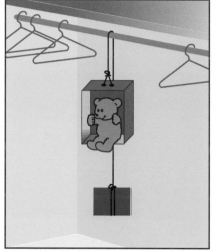

What You Need

Shoebox
Scissors
Clothesline about 8 feet (2.4 meters) long
Closet rod in a closet
Toys or a stuffed animal
Books about the same weight as the box
An adult to help

What You Do

1. Ask an adult to poke two holes in one end of the shoebox with the scissors. The holes should be about 2 inches (5 centimeters) apart.
2. Put one end of the clothesline through the two holes and tie a knot outside of the box. The box is your elevator car.
3. Place the free end of the clothesline over the closet rod. The closet rod is like a pulley. Place the toys in the elevator car and try to lift it.
4. Tie the free end of the clothesline to the books so the books hang vertically. The books should balance the box.
5. Put your toys in the elevator car. Pull down on rope. Try raising and lowering the elevator car to different heights.

The books act as a counterweight for the elevator car. The weights of the car and the counterweight are equal. You only have to lift the weight of the toys. Elevators in tall buildings also use counterweights. The elevator motor only has to lift the weight of the people because the counterweight and car are balanced.

Words to Know

boom (BOOM)—a fixed pole or beam

complex (kahm-PLEKS)—made of many parts

counterweight (KOWN-ter-WAYT)—a weight that balances a load

endless chain (END-less CHAYN)—a loop that connects two fixed pulleys

escalator (ESS-kuh-lay-tur)—a moving staircase that people ride to get from one level to another

force (FORSS)—anything that changes the speed, direction, or motion of an object

load (LOHD)—something that is moved

Read More

Glover, David. *Pulleys and Gears.* Simple Machines. Crystal Lake, Ill.: Rigby Interactive Library, 1997.

Hodge, Deborah. *Simple Machines.* Toronto: Kids Can Press, 1996.

Royston, Angela. *Pulleys and Gears.* Machines in Action. Chicago: Heinemann Library, 1997.

Internet Sites

Inventors Toolbox: Simple Machines
http://www.mos.org/sln/Leonardo/InventorsToolbox.html
School Zone, Simple Machines
http://www.science-tech.nmstc.ca/maindex.cfm?idx=1394&language=english&museum=sat&function=link&pidx=1394
Simple Machines
http://www.fi.edu/qa97/spotlight3/spotlight3.html

Index